NOËL 2002.

TO: DERRICK & SHARON,
MATTHEW & DANIEL.

WITH LOVE Julien

A taste of
Birmingham

First published 2002
by Midland Independent Magazines
28 Colmore Circus, Birmingham B4 6AX

ISBN 0-9543388-0-4

Editor: Fiona Alexander
Design Editor: Stacey Barnfield
Copy Editors: Jon Perks, Louise Palfreyman
Production Manager: Julia Gregory
Sales Manager: Leah Edmunds

Printed by William Gibbons and Sons Ltd., Willenhall, West Midlands

A ⟩ Trinity Mirror business

A taste of
Birmingham

Photography by Craig Holmes

CONTENTS

All dishes are based on a serving of four, unless otherwise stated.

FOREWORD by Didier Philipot

A Taste of Birmingham: what tastes and cooking trends represent this ever-changing city in the 21st century?

Traditionally, Birmingham has been the home of the balti and Indian fare. Perhaps not the first choice of location when considering that romantic dinner or important business luncheon. More likely, some of the luxurious country house hotels in the surrounding counties would have sprung to mind. But slowly new influences, famous names and more diverse cuisine have found a foothold here; from Mexican to Mongolian, and even classical French – every taste is now catered for.

Throughout my 11 years in England, I have watched Birmingham transform from a tired industrial city where dining out was regarded as a luxury, to an attractive, modern and vibrant venue packed with bars, restaurants and brasseries.

Birmingham is a city for the future with excellent amenities, a good infrastructure and home to a vast range of cultures. I truly hope that the enjoyment and pleasure derived from going out for a meal will continue to grow with the city and its people.

Diners now understand far more about the quality of the meals they are eating... and paying for. Perhaps we have the celebrity chefs and hours of cookery television programmes to thank for this! Nevertheless it is a positive step forward. People enjoy cooking and experimenting with new flavours and I hope this book will expand that knowledge and encourage more people to try something a little different.

A taste of
Birmingham

Your table is ready...

BANK

BANK

Bank Restaurant & Bar first opened in 1999 with the aim of providing fresh, robust and creative food with a twist on the classics.

Open breakfast, lunch and dinner, Bank is a lively urban brasserie, driven by our passion for food, pride in our service and our desire to offer simplicity at its best.

The kitchen is at the heart of Bank, creating a style of food that transcends fashion, fired by the imagination of a team whose professional attention to detail strives for intensity of flavours and consistency.

Bank classics include starters such as chicken & shrimp nam rolls, simple mains such as sausage and mash, and warm chocolate Valrhona cake with white chocolate ice cream for dessert. Headed by Executive Chef, David Colcombe, our kitchen runs the popular Bank School of Cookery for customers with an appetite to learn more about cooking.

Sister of London's award-winning Bank Aldwych and Bank Westminster, Bank Birmingham is the first venture outside London for our independent restaurant group. We are delighted to have been selected by local public opinion as 'Best Restaurant' 2002 Birmingham Nightlife Awards and to be recognised as part of the fabric of the city.

Bank is, essentially, a celebration of food and the theatre of dining.

www.bankrestaurants.com

Ann Tonks,
Marketing Director

Seared tuna, feta, tomato and pepper salad

INGREDIENTS

175g tuna	10g red onions
60g diced feta cheese	1g black cracked pepper
10g cucumber	10g green capsicum peppers
5ml mixed salad dressing (20ml olive oil,	10g yellow capsicum peppers
20ml white wine vinegar, 5g mustard)	1g fine table salt
15g mixed lettuce leaves	10g plum tomatoes
10ml Italian virgin olive oil	
5g black pitted olives	

METHOD

Peel peppers and cut into strips. Peel cucumber cut in half lengthways, scoop out seeds and cut into large slices. Peel onion and cut into large dice. Mix with feta, black olives, tomatoes and mixed salad, dress lightly and build it up in centre of plate. Pan fry tuna quickly, 10 seconds on each side. Slice and place around salad.

Confit duck leg, sauté potatoes, sauce vierge

INGREDIENTS

Confit duck leg	**Salt marinade**	**Sauce vierge**
1 portion duck leg	Sea salt	40g chopped shallots
30g pak choi	Sprig picked rosemary	20g each basil, tarragon, chives
80g new potatoes	Sprig picked thyme	
1 tin of duck fat	Peeled garlic	15g plum tomatoes
30g baby spinach	Juniper berry	15g each of green, red, yellow capsicum peppers
		200ml fresh olive oil
		10ml sherry vinegar
		5g fine table salt
		5g white ground pepper

METHOD

Sauce vierge: Peel peppers, finely dice. Blanch tomatoes, deseed and dice. Peel and finely chop shallots, sweat off, add vinegar and slowly whisk in oil. Add herbs and tomatoes to finish.

Salt marinade: Liquidise all ingredients together.

Salt legs for 24 hours. Remove salt and wash lightly under running water. Place in warm duck fat and cook for 45 minutes-1 hour until tender. Remove and chill until required. Trim fat round top bone for presentation.
Sauté new potatoes, until golden brown on each side, add pak choi and baby spinach at last moment and wilt slightly. Season with salt and pepper.
Place sauce vierge around outside of duck.

Chocolate and coconut parfait

INGREDIENTS

Parfait

125g sugar

35g water

75g egg yolk

100ml double cream – semi whipped

75g dark chocolate

Basic vanilla sponge

150g eggs (3, at room temperature)

150g caster sugar

150g soft flour

Vanilla essence

Coconut sorbet

500g coconut cream

75g sugar

Lemon zest

Rum chantilly cream

Sugar decoration

Chocolate sauce, vanilla sauce and papaya

Coconut shavings

METHOD

Parfait: Whip the yolks until light and foamy in food mixer. Dissolve sugar into water, boil until 118ºC (soft ball stage) with the food mixer still running slowly. Pour the hot syrup onto the yolks, continue whipping until cool. Add melted chocolate, then the semi whipped cream.

Sorbet: Add all ingredients together, churn using ice cream maker according to the manufacturers' directions.

Sponge: Prepare baking sheet by lining with greaseproof paper. Whisk the egg/sugar until it becomes thick and white in colour, add vanilla. Blend in the sieved flour that must be done with great care so as not to break down the light structure. Deposit mixture onto prepared baking sheet and spread level approximately 2mm in depth. Bake at 200ºC until light golden in colour. Remove from oven and sprinkle with sugar.

Using a metal ring cut out 4 circles from a sheet of vanilla sponge, place a ball of coconut sorbet into the centre of the metal ring, leaving a 2mm space around the sorbet. Pour the chocolate parfait mixture over the sorbet to the top of the ring, freeze for 2 hours. Whilst the parfaits are setting whip a little double cream with sugar and rum to taste, refrigerate.

Presentation: After 2 hours remove the parfaits, take a little of the chocolate sauce and finish the top with a thin layer, place the ring into the centre of a cold plate. Remove the metal ring using a dessert spoon, place a spoonful of rum chantilly on top of the chocolate. Finish with the sugar décor and mint leaf. Arrange the three sauces around the parfait and attach dried coconut shavings.

BRIAN TURNER'S

BRIAN TURNER'S

For the past few years, I have been a frequent visitor to the NEC, appearing at the Good Food Show and various exhibitions. So when I was invited to open Turner's at the new Crowne Plaza Hotel in a beautiful setting, I was delighted.

The restaurant, contemporary in design with furnishings in ochre, brown and orange is complemented with panoramic views of the al fresco terrace and Pendigo Lake beyond. Turner's working in partnership with Crowne Plaza have created a great restaurant that serves good value, simple food using a stream of great British produce that is inventive, tasty and well presented.

Gerard O'Sullivan is the executive chef who cooks in a 'Turner' style along with his team, many of whom worked with Gerard in the past. Many of the recipes are a variation on well-known or familiar recipes – the upmarket trifle 'white chocolate and raspberries' has been a favourite in my home for years.

Manfred Mai, restaurant manager, together with his assistants, have assembled a focused team of individuals, many of whom are from the local area. Together we aim to show that the hotel's restaurant and banqueting rooms can provide an exciting dining experience equal to the very best and one which we, at the Crowne Plaza Hotel NEC, are very proud.

Brian Turner, CBE

Smoked salmon and prawn slice with a chilli and lime dressing

Smoked salmon and prawns served separately were stalwarts for the Savoy first courses. This marriage of the two probably didn't work for the Savoy clients at that time, and would have been considered slightly adventurous. But it works wonderfully well now, particularly with the addition of the chilli and lime in the dressing, which are very much flavours of today.

INGREDIENTS

4 large slices smoked salmon, about 300g (10oz) in weight

115g (4oz) Philadelphia cream cheese

8 cooked giant Mediterranean prawns, shelled

2 tsps olive oil

1 tsp white wine vinegar

1 tbsp chopped fresh chives

Salt and freshly ground black pepper

12 whole chives

Chilli and lime dressing

½ fresh red chilli, seeded and finely chopped

Zest and juice of lime

2 tbsp soy sauce

4 tbsp olive oil

1 tbsp chopped fresh parsley

1 garlic clove, peeled and crushed

½ tsp caster sugar

METHOD

Cut 8 x 5cm (2 inch) circles from the four slices of smoked salmon. Chop the rest of the salmon, and mix with the cream cheese. Chop the prawns finely, and mix into the cheese. Whisk the oil and vinegar together, then mix into the cheese along with the chopped chives, salt and pepper. Leave to one side.

Have ready 4 x 5cm (2 inch) metal rings. Lay one circle of salmon in the bottom of each ring. Spoon some of the cheese mixture on top and pat it flat. Lay another circle of salmon on top, and pat that flat as well. Chill to set.

To make the dressing, mix the chilli with the lime zest, lime juice, soy sauce and olive oil. Add the parsley, garlic and sugar, and season with salt and pepper.

Carefully remove the salmon shapes from their rings, and arrange in the centre of each plate. Drizzle the dressing around, using the whole chives as a garnish.

BRIAN TURNER'S

Crowne Plaza Birmingham NEC, Pendigo Way, The NEC, Birmingham B40 1PS
Tel: 0121 781 4200

Long-cooked shoulder of lamb

INGREDIENTS

1 lamb shoulder 1.25-1.5kg, boneless	2 bay leaves
1 large onion, chopped	1 glass red wine
1 large carrot, chopped	1.5l lamb or beef stock
3 sprigs rosemary	Salt and freshly ground white pepper
2 cloves garlic finely chopped	2 tbsps ground nut/vegetable oil
3 sprigs thyme	

METHOD

Take the shoulder of lamb (which is boneless) and remove any large pieces of fat. Season with salt and pepper, a little chopped rosemary and chopped garlic.

Roll into a cylinder shape and secure tightly with string (your butcher will do it for you if you ask).

In a large pan, heat the oil until it starts to glisten, season the exterior of the lamb shoulder and brown gently on all sides. Place in the casserole dish.

In the same pan add the chopped onions and carrots and gently soften until golden brown, remove and add to the lamb in the casserole.

Keeping the pan warm, drain any fat and put the pan on to the heat, add the red wine and scrape (déglace) the pan lifting all the tasty morcels. As the wine reduces, add the stock and bring to the boil.

Pour the stock over the lamb, add the rosemary, thyme and bay leaves.

The lamb is cooked when it is soft to the touch. Allow to cool overnight, the fat on the stock will set on top so it is removed easily.

Slice into 2-3cm thick slices and re-heat gently in the oven in some of the reserved cooking stock (juices).

Serve with either hotpot potatoes or mash and some glazed carrots.

BRIAN TURNER'S

Crowne Plaza Birmingham NEC, Pendigo Way, The NEC, Birmingham B40 1PS
Tel: 0121 781 4200

White chocolate and raspberry trifle

Trifle used to be the staple dessert of families in the 1940s and 1950s, and was quite simple. Now we've moved on again, and here we have the richness of white chocolate, unheard of 40 years ago. This is the one where everyone cleans the plate.

INGREDIENTS

175g (6oz) white chocolate

2 medium egg yolks

25g (1oz) caster sugar

150ml milk

85ml (3fl oz) double cream

2$\frac{1}{2}$ tbsps icing sugar

4 x 4cm (1$\frac{1}{2}$ inch) slices Swiss roll (bought or home made)

2 tbsps Kirsch liqueur

225g (8oz) fresh raspberries

A few fresh mint sprigs

METHOD

Put a 55g (2oz) piece of the white chocolate in the fridge; this will make it easier to grate later. Break the remainder into small pieces.

Cream the egg yolks and caster sugar together in a large bowl. Whisk for about 2-3 minutes, until the mixture is pale, thick, creamy and leaves a trail.

Pour the milk and cream into a small, heavy based saucepan and bring to the boil. Pour on the egg yolk mixture, whisking all the time. Pour back into the pan and place over a moderate heat. Stir the mixture with a wooden spoon until it starts to thicken and coats the back of the spoon. Add the broken-up pieces of chocolate and stir in until completely incorporated. Remove the pan from the heat and allow to cool slightly. Cover the custard with a little icing sugar and a piece of clingfilm to prevent a skin forming.

Place the Swiss roll slices in a large glass bowl and sprinkle with the Kirsch. Scatter with fresh raspberries, reserving a few for decoration. Pour the white chocolate custard over the Swiss roll and leave to set in the fridge, preferably overnight.

To serve, decorate the trifle with the reserved raspberries. Take the piece of white chocolate from the fridge and finely grate over the trifle. Finally, dust with a little icing sugar and place the mint sprigs on top. You could make individual trifles – Martini glasses are good.

BRIAN TURNER'S
Crowne Plaza Birmingham NEC, Pendigo Way, The NEC, Birmingham B40 1PS
Tel: 0121 781 4200

CAFÉ IKON

CAFÉ IKON

When Ikon Gallery moved to Brindleyplace in 1998, the area was still underdeveloped. With an opportunity to provide contemporary food in the new award-winning building, James and his colleagues devised a menu that would look good on a plate; that could involve new exciting flavours in a smart contemporary arena with no pretensions of effect.

Following extensive research into the undeveloped style of Spanish tapas and raciones – where a few dishes could be shared using authentic ingredients with a slightly different twist, the café has become home to a loyal following of artists, performers, media folk, art enthusiasts, educationalists, food enthusiasts and Spanglophiles.

I am very proud that in our opening four years we have retained a loyal staff and been complimented by the repeat business of a great number of our customers; friends.

To all new customers who apologise for making a mess, we say don't worry – messy food cuts down a great social barrier – leading to enjoyment, which is after all why we are here.

James Marsden,
Proprietor

CAFÉ IKON

Pollo con pimientos

Pollo con pimientos is a favourite dish at Café Ikon. It combines the favourite flavours of Spanish cuisine with one of the classic sauces – Romesco sauce, which is an excellent accompaniment to many other dishes.

Pepper sauce

6 red peppers, grilled, skinned and deseeded	2 red chillies, diced
	1 bay leaf
1 onion, chopped and finely diced	1 stick of celery, diced
2 cloves of garlic, peeled and mashed	500ml vegetable or chicken stock

Combine all the ingredients into a saucepan, bring to the boil and simmer for 20 minutes. Reduce the stock by one half, remove from the hob and allow to cool. Blitz the sauce with a stick blender and you should have a vibrant red, thick pepper sauce.

Romesco sauce

250g toasted almonds (fat, skinless marcona almonds are best)	2 nora dried peppers – soaked for 1 hour
	200g tin of wood roasted peppers
200g breadcrumbs from a good day-old bread (pan de campagne)	10g sweet Spanish paprika
	150-250ml mild extra virgin olive oil

Put the first 5 ingredients into a food processor with the s-blade and blend, slowly drizzling the olive oil mixture until you have a thick, nutty paste. The amount of oil you use depends on the absorbency of the breadcrumbs. The sauce is best left for 2-3 days before use so the almonds and nora pepper flavour the whole mix.

Pollo con pimientos

4 6-8oz chicken breast fillets – skinless, cut into strips and marinated in garlic, fresh thyme and dry white wine for 1 hour	1 glass dry white wine
	200ml pepper sauce
	200ml double cream
25g butter	50g Romesco sauce

Gently poach the marinated chicken in its marinade along with the butter and a second glass of wine. After about 5 minutes add the pepper sauce and double cream and reduce for about 5 minutes on a medium flame. As the sauce reduces add the Romesco sauce which will then thicken the dish. Transfer these 4 portions to separate raciones dishes and top with extra Romesco, reserved wood smoked pepper strips and some fresh thyme. Serve with fresh bread, a light salad or patatas.

CAFÉ IKON

Ikon Gallery, 1 Oozells Sq., Brindleyplace, Birmingham B1 2HS
Tel: 0121 248 3226

Paella mixta

INGREDIENTS

2 cloves chopped garlic	6 raw tiger prawns
½ Spanish onion finely chopped	200g Calasparra rice
1 red pepper seeded and diced	1 morcilla (Spanish black sausage – optional)
1 tomato skinned, chopped and seeded	
2 anchovy fillets	12 black shell mussels
250ml sofrit or passata	2 langoustine
1 chorizo sausage cut into about 10 discs	1 oyster (optional)
1 chicken fillet (skinless), sliced into strips	1 glass dry white
300g cleaned fresh squid sliced into strips	500ml good hot fish/chicken stock with a pinch of saffron infused into it.

METHOD

In a paellera, cazuela or flat based pan with a short lip, fry off the first 5 ingredients in a little olive oil until the pepper and tomato are soft and the anchovy fillets have melted into the vegetable mix. Add the sofrit, chorizo, chicken, squid and prawns for about 3-5 minutes, until the chicken has sealed and the chorizo starts to impart its characteristic flavour.

Add the rice and stir the mixture around and loosen all these ingredients with the white wine. Add half the stock and stir – allow to cook for 5 minutes and then add the second half of the stock.

Pile the mussels, langoustine, oyster and morcilla onto the rice and cover and allow to cook on a low flame (or in a hot oven) for about 20 minutes. Let the paella stand for about 5 minutes after cooking, then dress the paella and serve with some chopped fresh parsley and wedges of lemon.

TIPS

Don't worry about the squid over-cooking, the paella cooking time is just right to return the squid to a lovely, soft texture.

CAFÉ IKON

Ikon Gallery, 1 Oozells Sq., Brindleyplace, Birmingham B1 2HS
Tel: 0121 248 3226

Pastel de trufa y chocolate

INGREDIENTS

500g good quality dark chocolate gently melted.

100g unsalted butter

400ml double cream – whipped to a soft peak

100g garrapinades (sugared almonds)

25ml strong black coffee – chilled

25ml brandy

METHOD

Add the butter to the melted dark chocolate. Roughly chop up or crush the sugared almonds and add the cooling chocolate mixture. Combine the whipped cream, coffee and brandy and when the chocolate is a cool liquid, fold into the cream. The praline should now resemble a mousse which can be dropped into an 8-inch square baking tin (lightly oiled) and refrigerated for two hours.

At the café we cut the cake into long fingers after standing in a warm area for 5 minutes and serve with more double cream and fresh fruit.

TIPS

Garrapinades are the gorgeous brown coated sugared almonds sold all around the Mediterranean but are quite difficult to find here. To make your own heat up 250g of caster sugar with a drop of cold water in a frying pan, as the sugar melts to a thick syrup, carefully add 200g of blanched almonds until coated. Turn the praline mixture onto a greased piece of tin foil and allow to chill. Then roughly chop this praline mixture and fold into the chocolate trying to retain some larger pieces of nuts.

CAFÉ LAZEEZ

CAFÉ LAZEEZ

Café Lazeez, regarded as 'Pioneers of New Wave Indian Cuisine', have been offering diners the opportunity to enjoy Indian food in a contemporary environment for over ten years.

The name has become synonymous with modern, elegant interiors, with all the restaurants boasting a visually exciting design and each site having a history behind it.

The multi award-winning and critically acclaimed menu includes traditional dishes made using only the very finest raw ingredients and fresh spices, offering the popular signature 'evolved dishes' such as Malabari pepper prawns as well as the more traditional Avadhi chicken korma and light bar snacks.

The emphasis is on light, fresh and healthy. All too often Indian cooking is excessively spicy, oily and rich.

At Lazeez frying is kept to a minimum and instead most of the dishes are grilled or dry-fried and olive oil is used in place of ghee, thus creating a selection of far healthier and lighter dishes than normally found at most Indian restaurants.

The Birmingham restaurant was the fourth in the group and the first to be opened outside the Capital. The Head Chef at Café Lazeez in Birmingham is Parvinder Multani, who previously worked at the Oberoi Hotel in Delhi. His innovative yet passionate approach to Indian cuisine is evident in the flavoursome and nourishing dishes he and his team create for you.

www.cafelazeez.com

CAFÉ LAZEEZ

Lamb seekh gilafi

INGREDIENTS

1.3kg lamb mince	1 tsp garam masala
1 onion	2 tsp coriander powder
1½ inch piece of ginger	4 green elaichi
1½ tsp garlic powder	4 green chilli
½ tsp chilli powder	½ bunch fresh coriander
1 tsp salt	1½ tsp whole jeera

METHOD

Preparation: Peel and chop the onion and reserve. Wash, scrape and finely chop the ginger. Wash and finely chop the fresh coriander leaves. Stalk and finely chop the green chillies.

Mix in all the ingredients and leave to rest in the refrigerator for half an hour. Prepare a small amount of the minced lamb in your hand. Roll onto a tandoori skewer. Cook under conventional grill until golden brown. Serve with chilled mint yoghurt.

CAFÉ LAZEEZ
116 Wharfside Street, The Mailbox, Birmingham B1 1RF
Tel: 0121 643 7979

Malabari peppered prawns

INGREDIENTS

12 tiger prawns
Salt
$1/2$ tsp white pepper powder
10 tsp tomato salsa
400ml coconut sauce

Accompaniments
600g saffron rice
12 raw banana wafers
12 fresh coriander sprigs

Tomato salsa
100g fresh tomatoes
200g tomato paste
50g colourful peppers
Pinch salt
2 tsp sugar
1 tsp vinegar
Dash Tabasco sauce
1 tsp chopped garlic

Coconut sauce
75ml oil
10-12 curry leaves

$1/2$ tsp mustard seeds
4-5 dried red chilies
110g onions
30g ginger paste
25g garlic paste
60g fresh tomatoes
15g salt
1 tsp red chilly powder
$1/2$ tsp turmeric
20g tamarind
400ml coconut milk
15g chopped coriander

METHOD

Preparation: Wash, slit and de-vein the prawns and leave the shell on. Make the tomato salsa as per the recipe. Marinate the prawns with salt, pepper and lemon juice. Fill the prawns (slit side) with the tomato salsa, about two spoons for each prawn. Make the coconut sauce as per the recipe. Make the banana wafers by slicing the raw banana lengthwise, then trimming the peel and crispy frying the banana slices making sure they do not bend. Wash and reserve sprigs of coriander. Make the saffron rice and keep aside.

Tomato Salsa: Roughly chop the fresh tomatoes. In a thick bottomed pan heat some oil. Fry the garlic till golden brown and then add the tomatoes and cook until they are well mashed. Add in the tomato paste, salt, sugar, Tabasco, and the vinegar and cook until you get the dropping consistency in the sauce. Add in the finely chopped peppers and finish cooking. Reserve until cool.

Coconut Sauce: In a pan heat some oil. Add in the mustard seeds and curry leaves and stir fry till they crackle. Add in the chopped onions and fry until golden. Stir in the ginger and garlic paste. Add in the powdered masala and the tomatoes. Add in the tamarind and the coconut milk and bring to a good boil. Finish cooking by adjusting the spices.

Method: Heat some oil in the pan and add the prawns with the salsa filled side facing upwards. Finish the cooking in the pre-heated moderate-to-hot oven.

Presentation: On a large dinner plate make of mound of saffron rice in the centre of the plate. Pour the coconut sauce around the rice. Place the oven-cooked prawns around the rice over the coconut sauce. Place the banana wafers and the sprigs of coriander around the rice alternating with the prawns.

CAFÉ LAZEEZ

Gajar ka halwa

INGREDIENTS

10kg carrots

2kg sugar

2.5kg khoa

400g pistachio

50ml rose water

20g green cardamom

750g ghee

METHOD

Preparation: Peel, wash and grate the carrots. Grate the khoa and keep aside. Poach and skin the pistachio and sliver them. Powder the green cardamom.

Dry roast the grated carrots in a heavy bottomed sauce pan until all the water has evaporated. Add sugar, ghee and cardamom powder and mix well continuing with the cooking. Add rose water, mix well and take off the heat.
Add the khoa and mix well. Serve hot with a scoop of vanilla ice cream.

CITY CAFÉ

CITY CAFÉ

Welcome to City Café, a quality modern British, yet affordable restaurant in the heart of Brindleyplace.

This fantastic venue with an ever-evolving menu is the perfect dining experience.

Head Chef at this restaurant with rooms is Martin Walker.

Martin joined the City Café in October 2000 prior to its opening in the following March. Previously sous chef at the original Bank restaurant in London, his vast experience includes a spell at Cézanne and the City of London Club as well as being Head Chef at the two AA rosette Cornish Cottage restaurant at Polzeath.

Together with Sous Chef Roger Gabor, Pastry Chef Elizabeth Farleigh and all his team, City Café is fast becoming known for some of the finest food in Birmingham.

Ham hock roulade with asparagus

If you can try and purchase free range rare breed pork it makes so much difference. Tamworth pork is the nearest to Birmingham. Couple it with another ingredient grown not far from Birmingham – asparagus from Evesham – and you have a dish to grace any table.

INGREDIENTS

2 ham hocks

2 carrots peeled and chopped

2 sticks of celery peeled and chopped

1 large onion peeled and chopped

2 bay leaves

½ bunch of thyme and rosemary

10 black peppercorns

Water

Roulade

2 shallots – finely chopped

50g parsley – chopped

50ml veal jus

50ml ham stock

50ml duck fat

To finish

1 bunch of asparagus peeled

1 head of frisée picked and washed

Aged balsamic vinegar

Cider dressing (see below)

Cider dressing

1 egg yolk

150ml groundnut oil

200ml cider – reduced to 1 tbsp

25ml cider vinegar (white wine vinegar can be used instead)

1 tsp of herb mustard

Salt and pepper

METHOD

Ham Hock: Place in pot and cover with water. Bring to boil and skim. Add the chopped vegetables, bay leaves, thyme and rosemary and bring back to the boil. Simmer for approximately 2 hours or until the meat comes away from the bone. Remove from liquid and cool for 30 minutes. Pick off meat and place in bowl with shallots, parsley, veal jus, ham stock and duck fat. Thoroughly mix. Roll in cling film to form roulade and leave in fridge to set for 24 hours.

Cider dressing: Whisk the egg yolk until it starts to thicken, add cider reduction, vinegar and mustard and keep whisking.
Slowly add the oil and season. The dressing should resemble a thin mayonnaise.

To serve: Chargrill the asparagus. Place 3 slices of the roulade in the middle of the plate. Dress the frisée with balsamic vinegar and season. Pile on top of the roulade. Finish with a couple of sticks of asparagus and cider dressing.

CITY CAFÉ

City Inn Birmingham, 1 Brunswick Sq., Brindleyplace, Birmingham B1 2HW
Tel: 0121 633 6300

Chargrilled swordfish, caper and olive oil salad with salsa verdi

A wonderful summer dish, swordfish can be easily barbecued as well. The lemon oil takes a while to make so see if your local deli stocks it.

INGREDIENTS

6 180g swordfish steaks	
2 baby gem lettuce	
20 extra fine capers	
10 petit luques olives – pitted and sliced	
Salsa verdi (see right)	
Lemon oil	

Salsa verdi

Half a bunch of parsley

10g mint leaves

$\frac{1}{2}$ lemon – juice and zest

$\frac{1}{2}$ clove of garlic finely chopped

$\frac{1}{2}$ tsp of capers

10ml extra virgin olive oil

Salt and pepper to taste

METHOD

Shred baby gem lettuce finely and place in a mixing bowl with capers and olives. Season with black pepper and salt and add a few drops of the lemon oil. Place the salad in the middle of the plate. Brush swordfish with olive oil and season. Chargrill swordfish according to taste (medium rare is best). Place fish on top of salad and finish with a small amount of the salsa verdi on top of the swordfish. Accompany with a tomato dressing and lemon oil.

Salsa verdi: Place parsley, mint, capers and garlic into a blender and mix. Add lemon juice and olive oil. Season to taste.

CITY CAFÉ

City Inn Birmingham, 1 Brunswick Sq., Brindleyplace, Birmingham B1 2HW
Tel: 0121 633 6300

CITY CAFÉ

Lemon posset with blueberries and banana compote

Posset, which originated in medieval times as a curdled milk drink, has developed into this smooth mousse-like dessert. You will need 6 margarita glasses.

INGREDIENTS

700g double cream
188g caster sugar
Zest of 1½ lemons
Juice of 4 lemons
1 large banana diced (keep 6 slices for decoration)

1 punnet of blueberries
2 tsps of sugar
Icing sugar

METHOD

Bring to boil cream, caster sugar and lemon zest. Remove from heat and add lemon juice and pass through a fine strainer. Dice banana and toss in icing sugar and lemon juice. Gently cook blueberries for a couple of minutes with the sugar.

To finish: Place a spoon of bananas in the base, then the blueberries and finally pour on the posset mix. Leave to set in the fridge for 2 hours.

Decorate with a slice of banana, a few blueberries and a sprig of mint.

CITY CAFÉ

City Inn Birmingham, 1 Brunswick Sq., Brindleyplace, Birmingham B1 2HW
Tel: 0121 633 6300

JYOTI

JYOTI

Although we won the 2002 Nightlife Best Balti Award, we're not a balti as such, just a normal traditional vegetarian restaurant.

We're vegetarians ourselves because we're a Hindu family so that was a big part of our growing up.

Apart from the kitchen and waiting staff, it's basically four of us – my brother Mukesh and myself and our wives Harsha and Bhavna who are the two main chefs.

We opened Jyoti (the name relates to the logo we have – it refers to the light that comes out of the flame) in September 1997; our late father, Govindji Joshi, to whom we dedicated our Overall Winner trophy at the Nightlife Awards 2002, first opened a sweet centre and café in Ladypool Road in 1976.

There aren't that many vegetarian restaurants out there, it's surprising, but there are so many new foods which a few years back you would not have been able to get hold of here and vegetarianism is a big market and it's getting bigger.

Our philosophy is simple; we believe if you offer quality food and good service and give value for money, people will come back.

Rajendra Joshi

Dahi wada

In Indian cuisine wadas are dumplings. They come in varying shapes and sizes and for this recipe are served in a yoghurt (dahi) sauce.

INGREDIENTS

1 cup coarse matpe (bean flour)	1 stem curry leaves
1 litre yoghurt	250ml oil
1 tbsp cumin powder	Salt to taste
2 green chillies	

METHOD

To make the dumplings soak the flour for five hours in water (enough to cover).
Swill and mix the resulting paste together until thick and soft.
Add salt, then form dumpling shapes with hands – aim for golf ball size.
Place in the palm of the hand, pat until round and make a hole in the centre.
Deep fry in the oil until light brown.

Allow to cool, soak the dumplings in the yoghurt for three hours, chop green chillies finely and sprinkle over with the cumin powder, salt and curry leaves. Serve.

JYOTI

569-571 Stratford Road, Sparkhill, Birmingham B11 4LS
Tel: 0121 766 7199

JYOTI

Vegetable biryani

INGREDIENTS

2 cups basmati rice

1 cup steamed vegetables (green peas, beans, cauliflower, carrots etc)

2 medium onions, chopped

2 tbsps raisins

2 tbsps cashew nuts or slivered almonds

2 tsps salt

1 tsp turmeric powder

$\frac{1}{2}$ tsp cinnamon powder

$\frac{1}{4}$ tsp each clove powder, nutmeg powder, chilli powder, coriander powder

3 tbsps butter

METHOD

Preheat the oven to 375ºF, gas mark 5.

Soak the basmati rice in water for 30 mins. Rinse and drain well. Melt half the butter in a frying pan and sauté the onions, cashew nuts and raisins until golden brown. Keep aside. Melt the rest of the butter in the pan and add the rice and fry until it is coated in the butter and not sticking together.

Add all the spices and mix well. Empty the rice into a baking pan, add salt and $1\frac{1}{2}$ cups of water. Place in the oven and cook for 20 mins or until rice is cooked.

Add the vegetables, onions, raisins and cashew nuts to the rice and mix well. Serve.

Roti Indian flatbread

INGREDIENTS

3 cups plain flour

1 tbsp vegetable oil

1 tsp salt

$1\frac{1}{2}$ cups hot water

Butter for frying, or vegetable oil

METHOD

Mix the flour, oil, salt and water to form a soft dough. Fold and knead about a dozen times, sprinkling with more water if too dry, or with more flour if too sticky. Roll the dough until about 5mm thick. Trim to circumference of frying pan (10 inch).

Heat the pan and cook the roti until brown, turning it over every 10-15 seconds. After a couple of minutes serve hot.

JYOTI

569-571 Stratford Road, Sparkhill, Birmingham B11 4LS
Tel: 0121 766 7199

Malai kofta

Koftas are the Indian version of meatballs. Here a vegetarian alternative is offered, using cheese (malai). This is a low fat cholesterol-free dish ready in 45 minutes.

INGREDIENTS

Koftas

100g low fat paneer, mashed

5 medium sized potatoes, steamed or baked and mashed

1 onion, chopped

$\frac{1}{2}$ tbsp raisins

5 finely chopped green chillies

1 inch root ginger crushed

$\frac{1}{2}$ tbsp chopped coriander leaves

2 tsps lime/lemon juice, fresh

$\frac{1}{2}$ tsp red chilli powder

Salt to taste

2 tbsps freshly grated coconut

2 tbsps grounded peanuts (plain)

Gravy

125g half fat cream

50g reduced fat paneer, grated

100g skimmed milk

1 onion, chopped

1 inch root ginger, crushed

2-3 cloves garlic, crushed

$\frac{1}{2}$ tbsp coriander leaves, chopped

$\frac{1}{2}$ cup half fat yoghurt

Spices for the gravy

1 tsp red chilli powder garam masala, coriander powder

$\frac{1}{2}$ tsp turmeric powder, cumin seeds

2 cardamom pods, remove shell

Salt to taste

1 tbsp Canola oil

3 chopped tomatoes (fresh)

Garnishing

1 tbsp grated paneer

$\frac{1}{2}$ tbsp chopped coriander

$\frac{1}{2}$ tbsp half fat cream

1 tbsp grated coconut

METHOD

Preheat the oven to 150ºC, gas mark 1.

Mix all the kofta ingredients together except the raisins. Make into small balls, putting 2-3 raisins in the centre. Put the koftas in the oven for 20 minutes at 260ºC.

Put the yoghurt in a bowl and mix together with the spices. Put aside.

Mix the remaining gravy ingredients (apart from the coriander leaves) in a blender until you have a smooth paste.

Heat a non-stick frying pan and add the oil. When it becomes hot add the yoghurt mixture and fry on medium heat, stirring all the time until a thick consistency is achieved and the oil separates out. Add the paste from the blender and fry for 5-7 minutes stirring well. Add 1$\frac{1}{2}$ cups water and simmer for 10 minutes. Mix in the chopped coriander leaves. Place the koftas in a bowl and pour the gravy over them.

JYOTI
569-571 Stratford Road, Sparkhill, Birmingham B11 4LS
Tel: 0121 766 7199

LA GALLERIA

LA GALLERIA

Ours was the first bistro style bar and restaurant in Birmingham.

We were also one of the first Italian restaurants in the city, in fact, in 1977, there weren't that many restaurants at all. People used to have to wait weeks for a reservation and we built up a reputation to be proud of. Of course, these days there's more competition, but that's not a bad thing. We have the edge as an authentic Italian family-run restaurant, where all the ingredients are bought in and cooked by ourselves.

Marcello is from South Italy, near Lecce, where food is still very much a central part of the culture, and our menu reflects this.

Over the years we have entertained all the big names from the theatre and sports world, local media and of course the people of Birmingham. We offer celebrities a quiet place where they can have a meal without any fuss. I remember when Bryan Robson came in, and we've served each of the Three Tenors, although not together unfortunately.

We have also held some memorable family events for our loyal clientele. We've had wedding receptions, christening parties – some of our customers remember coming here as young couples and now bring their children.

The recipes we have chosen reflect our preference for natural down-to-earth ingredients. People want recipes they can actually cook, that they can try at home, rather than reading cookery books for entertainment.

Marcello and Kay Manca

LA GALLERIA

Pepper salad with capers

Preparation time 30 minutes plus 1 hour refrigeration

INGREDIENTS

3 large peppers (1 red, 1 green, 1 yellow)

6 tbsps olive oil

1 clove of garlic peeled and finely chopped

Basil leaves, roughly chopped

Fresh marjoram, roughly chopped

2 tbsps capers

1 tbsp white wine vinegar

METHOD

Cut peppers in half, remove core and seeds. Press with the back of a knife to flatten. Brush the skin side with olive oil and place on a tray under a pre-heated grill.

Grill until skin is charred.

Remove, and place in to a plastic bag and leave for a few minutes. Then, carefully remove skin. Cut peppers into strips and arrange in groups according to colour on a serving dish (a white background looks effective).

Scatter chopped garlic, herbs and capers over top. Mix together the remaining olive oil with the vinegar and salt and a good grind of black pepper. Pour over salad.

Refrigerate for 1 hour before serving. Serve with crusty bread, olive oil and balsamic vinegar.

LA GALLERIA

Restaurant & Wine Bar Bistro, Paradise Place, Birmingham B3 3HJ

Tel: 0121 236 1006

LA GALLERIA

Bistecca pizzaiola

INGREDIENTS

4 lean sirloin steaks (can use fillet)

1 jar of passata (available in good supermarkets)

1 clove of crushed garlic

1 onion finely chopped

Large tbsp olive oil

Pinch of oregano

20 capers and 4 anchovy fillets (chopped together)

Half glass of red wine

Salt and pepper

METHOD

Heat olive oil in a pan. Add onions and garlic and fry until golden brown. Add passata, wine, capers, anchovies and salt and pepper. Simmer on a low heat for 20 minutes.

Grill or pan fry steaks to your personal liking, then place in sauce. Simmer for a few minutes.

Serve with crisp salad and new potatoes.

LA GALLERIA

Restaurant & Wine Bar Bistro, Paradise Place, Birmingham B3 3HJ
Tel: 0121 236 1006

LA GALLERIA

Tiramisu

1 packet of boudoir biscuits	6 large fresh eggs
Half pint of strong black coffee	4oz white sugar
2 tbsps of Marsala wine	1 oblong deep dish
2 packets mascarpone cheese (approx 500g each)	

METHOD

You will need three bowls. Separate eggs and whisk whites until stiff. Add yolks and sugar to cheese and mix together thoroughly.

Add Marsala to coffee.

Carefully dip biscuits into coffee mixture – line the base of your dish with the coffee soaked biscuits. Now mix together both egg mixtures carefully with a metal spoon. Place a layer on top of biscuits. Repeat process until biscuits and mixture are finished.

Sprinkle with chocolate powder or grate chocolate on top. Place in the fridge for at least an hour to set.

Serve with double cream and fresh strawberries.

LA GALLERIA

Restaurant & Wine Bar Bistro, Paradise Place, Birmingham B3 3HJ
Tel: 0121 236 1006

LA TOQUE D'OR

LA TOQUE D'OR

Cooking has taken me all over the world, from Sun City in South Africa to Indonesia, Paris and even the Lake District. But after living in England for over 11 years, I now feel truly settled in this country.

After five and a half years as the Head Chef at Brockencote Hall Hotel, Chaddesley Corbett, where I was awarded three Rosettes by the AA, I felt the need to pursue my own venture, and now, 18 months later La Toque D'Or has been awarded the top rating of five stars in both The Birmingham Post and Metro newspapers and is generally regarded as one of the best places to dine in Birmingham for quality food and original, inventive dishes.

Cooking good food is about using the best and freshest ingredients possible, and keeping the dish simple and natural. Of course, you must enjoy eating as well so that your appreciation and personal passion for the food passes into the final dish.

I hope you enjoy experimenting with my recipes. Happy cooking and bon appetit!

Didier Philipot

LA TOQUE D'OR

Honey roasted lamb sweetbreads, sautéed
girolle mushrooms, Cumbrian air-dried ham,
honey and lovage flavoured jus

INGREDIENTS

12 pieces of lamb sweetbreads	10ml of brown chicken jus
4 slices of Cumbrian air-dried ham	2 leaves of lovage
20 small girolle mushrooms	2 knobs of unsalted butter
2 tablespoons of clear honey	Salt, pepper
1 clove of garlic	Extra virgin olive oil

METHOD

Trim the sweetbreads of any fat and skin, and then rinse in plenty of cold water,
changing the water several times until it runs clear.

Cut each slice of ham into 5 regular pieces.

Bring 1 spoonful of honey to the boil with the clove and brown chicken jus and
simmer for a few minutes.

Season and pan-fry the sweetbreads in a non-stick pan with oil. Colour on both
sides, add the remaining honey and caramelise.

Sauté the girolle mushrooms in butter. Shred the lovage as fine as possible. Add to
the honey jus at the last minute and serve.

TIPS

The sweetbreads should remain slightly pink as they will become rubbery if
overcooked. Do not over-infuse the lovage in the jus as it is a very strong-tasting
herb and will overpower the whole dish.

LA TOQUE D'OR
27 Warstone Lane, Hockley, Birmingham B18 6JQ
Tel: 0121 233 3655

LA TOQUE D'OR

Caramelised Isle of Skye king scallops, tomato confit, green asparagus, basil butter sauce

20 large, hand-dived king scallops	1 lemon
10 vine plum tomatoes	Sea salt, black pepper, sugar
20 asparagus spears	1 sprig of thyme
1 bunch of basil	Extra virgin olive oil
½ pack of unsalted butter	

METHOD

Remove the skins from the tomatoes. Cut them in half, removing any water or seeds. Sprinkle both sides with salt, pepper, sugar, thyme and oil. Bake in a very low oven for 2 hours – gas mark 3 or 4.

Rinse every scallop under running water to get rid of any sand. Cook asparagus in plenty of boiling salted water and refresh in ice-cold water. Boil a little water and lemon juice together with salt and pepper. Whisk in butter, bit by bit, while keeping a homogeneous sauce. Keep warm.

Pan-fry the scallops in olive oil in a non-stick pan until caramelised on one side only. Bring butter sauce to the boil. Add basil leaves and blend until smooth. Pass through a fine sieve and check the seasoning.

Warm the asparagus in a little foaming butter and serve.

TIPS

Ask your fishmonger for hand-dived scallops, he will prepare them for you. Don't settle for pre-cut scallops soaked in brine, as they will be flavourless and rubbery. If the scallops are caramelised on one side, no further cooking is required. If they lose their juices, they lose their taste. Keep the asparagus 'al dente'.

LA TOQUE D'OR
27 Warstone Lane, Hockley, Birmingham B18 6JQ
Tel: 0121 233 3655

Roasted yellow peach with lavender, bitter chocolate blinis, pistachio ice cream

INGREDIENTS

Blinis

100g extra bitter chocolate

25g butter

25g egg yolk

100g egg white

30g caster sugar

Peach

4 yellow peaches

30g butter

20g sugar

1 vanilla pod

1 sprig of lavender

Juice of $\frac{1}{2}$ a lemon

METHOD

Melt chocolate and butter in a bain-marie. Add egg yolks and stir well. Whisk egg whites into stiff peaks and add caster sugar to make a meringue.
Fold both the chocolate mixture and the meringue mixture together, keeping it as airy as possible. Keep in fridge.

Cut the peaches into 8 regular segments. Melt the butter in a non-stick pan. Add peaches, sugar, lemon juice, vanilla seeds. Caramelise, then add the lavender and leave to infuse.
Bake 4 large chocolate blinis at 200°C for 4 minutes. Arrange the peaches in a circle on a plate. Place the hot blini in the centre and top with pistachio ice cream. Pour the juice around the peaches.

LA TOQUE D'OR
27 Warstone Lane, Hockley, Birmingham B18 6JQ
Tel: 0121 233 3655

LE PETIT BLANC

LE PETIT BLANC

We opened Le Petit Blanc brasserie in Birmingham in August 1999. I arrived in the UK in 1972 with a passion for food and cooking which stems from my traditional French roots, where the heart of the family is the dining table and I wanted to recreate this environment for everyone to enjoy.

My aim was to create a brasserie offering simple and wholesome French food using the freshest seasonal ingredients at a price most people could afford. The result was 'Le Petit Blanc'; of which I am very proud.

Since opening, we have become renowned for offering top quality contemporary French cuisine which has been acknowledged through numerous awards and accolades including two AA rosettes and a Michelin Bib Gourmand.

Our executive chef Clive Fretwell (having worked as my head chef at Le Manoir for 15 years) has joined forces with me and works alongside Le Petit Blanc kitchen team.

Le Petit Blanc reflects the cosmopolitan, lively atmosphere of Birmingham which has developed into an international business centre and successful city with European status. We are a brasserie in the truest sense; open throughout the day with a menu designed to suit every occasion. Pop in for a glass of champagne, a Blanc vite quick single dish, a family lunch or a leisurely three-course dinner. We welcome everyone, families too, and offer fresh 'real food' dishes on our children's menu and a fun activity pack, whilst our two private dining rooms cater for receptions, celebrations and business meetings.

A true eating experience of course starts with the food but can only be enhanced by a culture of welcome and hospitality achieved through complete team work. The success of a great restaurant is about people and the team at Le Petit Blanc are amongst the very best.

We very much look forward to welcoming you.

Raymond Blanc

Goats' cheese deep fried

INGREDIENTS

2 sheets spring roll pastry

200g goats' cheese, Saint Loup

16g tapenade

1 egg

Tapenade

25g black olives, stoned

6g anchovy fillets, tinned

12g capers, drained and washed

1 clove garlic, peeled and crushed

10ml extra virgin olive oil

METHOD

Cut each sheet of the spring roll pastry into 4, cover with a damp cloth. Slice the goats' cheese logs into 4 x 50g portions. Place 4g of tapenade onto each portion of goats' cheese. Brush two squares of spring roll pastry with egg wash. Lay one square on top of the other at 45 degree angle. Place one goats' cheese onto the middle of the sheet, tapenade side down.

Fold the first sheet carefully over the goats' cheese ensuring all the seams are properly sealed. Repeat with second sheet.

Tapenade: Purée all ingredients until very smooth. Will keep one month if refrigerated.

LE PETIT BLANC

Nine Brindleyplace, Birmingham B1 2HS

Tel: 0121 633 7333

Seabream fillet, bouillabaisse sauce

INGREDIENTS

4 black seabream fillets
40ml extra virgin olive oil
120ml bouillabaisse sauce
120g rouille sauce
640g potatoes saffron fondants
320g roasted red peppers
2g salt
1g white coarse grained pepper

Bouillabaisse sauce
0.3g seabream carcass, washed and chopped into 3cm dice
60ml extra virgin olive oil
60g Spanish onions, peeled and cut into 1cm dice
60g fennel chopped 1cm dice

9g garlic, peeled and crushed
I pkt saffron pure powder
1g chopped thyme
A bay leaf
3.5g salt
24g tomato purée
60g plum tomatoes, roughly chopped
75ml white cooking wine, boiled for 10 seconds
240ml water
7.5ml Pernod
30ml extra virgin olive oil

Sauce rouille
1 egg yolk
8g crushed garlic
1 pkt saffron pure powder
100ml extra virgin olive oil

1g salt
1 pinch cayenne

Potatoes saffron fondants
1kg salad potatoes
25ml extra virgin olive oil
50g finely chopped shallots
70ml water
2g thyme
2 x 50g bay leaves
1 pkt saffron pure powder
10g salt

Roasted red peppers
330g sweet red peppers
33ml extra virgin olive oil
6.6g crushed garlic
9.9ml white wine vinegar
6.6g salt

METHOD

In a hot frying pan seal the seabream flesh side down in the olive oil. Turn the fish over and continue cooking skin side down until cooked. Season the flesh with lemon juice, salt and pepper. Re-heat the fondant potatoes (see separate recipe) in the oven for 5 minutes until hot throughout. In a hot pan re-heat the roasted red peppers until hot. In a hot pan bring the bouillabaise sauce to the boil, remove from heat. Whisk in the rouille.

Bouillabaisse sauce: On a low heat sweat fennel, garlic, saffron, thyme and bayleaf in the 60ml olive oil for 5 minutes without colouring. Add the fish bones, continue to cook for a further 10 minutes. Add the purée, tomatoes, white wine and water. Bring to the boil, skim. Reduce heat and simmer for 30 minutes, skimming well. Add Pernod. Liquidise coarsely, pass through a fine chinois. Finish by blitzing in 30ml olive oil. Label, date and refrigerate.

Rouille sauce: Whisk together the egg yolks, garlic and saffron powder. Slowly add the olive oil, whisking all the time. Add salt and cayenne pepper. Name, label, date and refrigerate.

Potatoes fondants: Prepare the potatoes into an ellipse shape. Sweat the shallots, thyme and bay leaves in the olive oil for 2 minutes. Add the water, potatoes, saffron powder and salt. Bring to a gentle boil, then simmer gently until almost cooked. Allow to cool in the cooking liquor.

Roasted red peppers: Cut red peppers in half, remove the pith and seeds. Roast in a hot oven 180ºC for 25 minutes with the olive oil and garlic until the skin has blistered. Add the white wine vinegar to deglaze. Place into a suitable container and cover with cling film. Allow to cool. Remove skin, reserve the peeled peppers in the cooking juices.

Dressing: Place the fondant potatoes onto the centre of the plate. Place the red peppers onto the fondants, top with sea bream. Spoon the sauce around.

LE PETIT BLANC
Nine Brindleyplace, Birmingham B1 2HS
Tel: 0121 633 7333

Soup red fruits and strawberry sorbet

INGREDIENTS

600ml soup red fruits

200g strawberry sorbet

160g strawberries

100g raspberries

80g blueberries

100g blackberries

4 mint sprigs

Red fruit soup

30ml water

30g caster sugar

600g strawberries

METHOD

Place the 150g of red fruit soup into a dessert bowl. Divide the red fruits between the four bowls, place into the centre of the dessert bowl. Place one scoop of strawberry sorbet on top of each bowl of fruit and decorate with a sprig of mint.

Red fruit soup: Bring the sugar and water to the boil for 1 minute then allow to cool. Place the strawberries into a liquidiser with the syrup and purée together. Refrigerate until required.

LE PETIT BLANC
Nine Brindleyplace, Birmingham B1 2HS
Tel: 0121 633 7333

LEITH'S

LEITH'S

Leith's is extremely proud to be associated with the Birmingham Hippodrome Theatre following the substantial re-development, which has ensured its status as one of the most prestigious and magical theatres in the country.

Leith's style and quality complements the high artistic standards incorporated into the newly-created culture of the theatre. A testament to this is the Leith's company motto of being 'Simply Better'.

We at Leith's believe in creating menus which are simple in concept but at the same time deliver quality and value for money.

The Hippodrome gets a vast cross section of people moving through its premises, so Leith's has to appeal to young, old and the more modern tastes.

Tim Goddard,
General Manager

Salmon with pear salsa

INGREDIENTS

Salmon

55g slices of salmon

1 sliced onion

Sliced carrots

2 bay leaves

Black peppercorn

5fl oz white wine vinegar

3 sticks of sliced celery

1l of water

Pear salsa

1 dessert pear, finely diced

1 small red onion, finely diced

4 plum tomatoes, seeded and diced

Sweet chilli sauce to bind

METHOD

Wash and peel carrots, cut into round slices, peel and roughly chop onion and celery. Place vegetables in a saucepan. Add water, white wine, bay leaves and crushed peppercorn. Bring to the boil and simmer for 20 minutes then leave to cool. Prepare salmon, remove skin and any bones. Cut salmon into thin slices (2 slices per portion).

Place salmon delice (slices) into cooking liquor, return to the heat and poach salmon for 5 minutes, remove salmon from cooking liquor, place on a tray to cool. Place in fridge.

Pear salsa: Mix all ingredients together to make a salsa.

To serve: Place salmon onto a starter plate with washed salad leaves, wedge of lemon, pear salsa and sweet chilli sauce to finish.

LEITH'S

Birmingham Hippodrome Theatre, Hurst Street, Birmingham B5 4TB
Tel: 0121 689 3181

Beef fillet

INGREDIENTS

Beef fillet	2 bay leaves
1 sliced onion	Crushed peppercorn
Thyme	Banana shallot
2 cloves of garlic	Butter
Red wine	Marinade red wine
3 tbsps brandy	Caster sugar

METHOD

Prepare the fillet of beef by discarding any fat or sinew. Prepare the marinade placing all ingredients together.

Place fillet of beef in marinade for about six hours.

Using the marinade make a red wine sauce.

Peel banana shallot, cut in half lengthways.

Melt butter in a pan, lay the shallot halves flat, (side down) in pan and sprinkle with sugar. Cook slowly on a low heat until they start to colour.

Add a little of the red wine sauce and cook until reduced.

The fillet steak may be chargrilled or pan fried to your liking. Rare steak $1\frac{1}{2}$ minutes each side. Medium steak $3\frac{1}{2}$ minutes each side.

To serve: Place the fillet of beef in the centre of a plate, place the caramelised shallot on top of the fillet and pour the sauce around. Serve with baby roast potatoes and seasoned vegetables.

LEITH'S

Birmingham Hippodrome Theatre, Hurst Street, Birmingham B5 4TB
Tel: 0121 689 3181

Summer berries with Kirsch sabayon

INGREDIENTS

500g assorted summer berries –
strawberry, raspberries, blackberries,
redcurrants and blueberries

Sabayon

3 egg yolks

3 tbsps of Kirsch or water

½ tsp cornflour

3oz sifted icing sugar

Balsamic syrup

100ml balsamic vinegar

50ml red wine

50g brown sugar

METHOD

Pick over the berries, wash and chill.

Make the sabayon. Place all the ingredients in a heat proof bowl, over a pan of simmering water. Whisk the mixture until it turns a pale cream colour, continue whisking to a stable foam. Remove the bowl from the heat and cool, whisking occasionally.

Just before serving, arrange the berries on a dessert plate.

Whisk the sabayon until thick, then spoon over berries. Using a blow torch, brown the sabayon. Serve immediately with a drizzle of balsamic syrup.

Balsamic syrup: Bring all the ingredients to boil in a saucepan, reducing until slightly sticky. Chill and serve over berries.

LEITH'S

Birmingham Hippodrome Theatre, Hurst Street, Birmingham B5 4TB
Tel: 0121 689 3181

METRO BAR AND GRILL

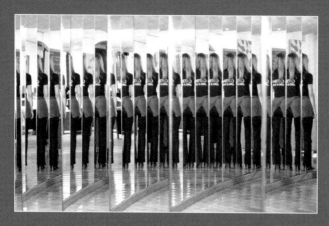

METRO BAR AND GRILL

It's been almost five years now since we set up Metro; at the time we didn't think there were many upmarket bars and restaurants in the city; we wanted a bustly atmosphere, somewhere you could come in for a business lunch or dinner, a romantic lunch or dinner or just pop in for a quick drink and bar snack.

I think we're very women-friendly – you see groups of businesswomen holding meetings here every day – it's not a male dominated environment – and what many customers probably don't realise is we have a lady head chef, Jenny Clarke, who's been with us since we started.

The menu, which is modern European, is changed three times a year, along with a daily fresh fish selection.

We also have an extensive wine and champagne list – one of the biggest in Birmingham.

Chris Kelly and Paul Salisbury

Basil cous cous pancakes with girolle mushrooms, baby leeks and roast cherry tomatoes

INGREDIENTS

100g plain flour	5 red and 5 yellow cherry tomatoes
2 whole eggs	12 baby leeks
1/4 pint milk	Basil mayonnaise
50g cous cous	1 sprig rosemary
1 bunch basil, chopped	Olive oil
Juice from 1/2 lemon	Truffle oil
Salt and pepper	Rocket leaves
200g girolle mushrooms	Salt and pepper

METHOD

Mix flour, eggs and milk to a smooth consistency. Pour boiling water over cous cous just to cover, cling film and leave to stand for 5 minutes or until the water is absorbed and cous cous is light and fluffy.

Mix the basil and lemon juice with the cous cous using a fork then add the cous cous to the batter, season and mix well.

Lightly oil a small frying or rosti pan, add 50g of the mix, cook on both sides to golden brown and repeat to leave 2 pancakes.

Place cherry tomatoes on a baking tray, drizzle with olive oil and rosemary, blister in a hot oven for 2 minutes.

Sauté the mushrooms in butter for 3 minutes. Blanch the leeks, place on a tray then drizzle with oil, season and place in hot oven for 2 minutes.

Assemble the dish as follows: use one pancake as base, add basil mayonnaise, dressed rocket, tomatoes and mushrooms, top with the second pancake, place the baby leeks on top and dress with a little truffle oil.

METRO BAR AND GRILL
73 Cornwall Street, Birmingham B3 2DF
Tel: 0121 200 1911

Roast skate with lobster, mango and chorizo kebab, rocket and aioli salad

INGREDIENTS

4 small skate wings

1 cooked lobster tail, thick slices

1/2 mango, diced

1 sweet potato, diced

2 small chorizo sausages

Butter

Basil leaves

Basil oil

Salt and pepper

Rocket leaves

5fl oz mayonnaise

5 garlic cloves

METHOD

Fillet the skate wings. Roast the sweet potato in a little olive oil with seasoning. Cook and slice the chorizo sausage.

Assemble kebabs alternating mango, potato, lobster, chorizo and basil leaves.

Prepare the aioli by mincing the garlic cloves with the mayonnaise.

Place the skate fillets on a baking tray, add a knob of butter and seasoning, bake at 180°C for 10 minutes.

Finish off the kebabs under a low-medium grill for 2-3 minutes. Dress the rocket with basil oil and season. Place on a small mound of aioli, place the skate fillet on the rocket and top with a kebab.

Drizzle some basil oil around the plate for decoration.

METRO BAR AND GRILL

73 Cornwall Street, Birmingham B3 2DF

Tel: 0121 200 1911

Nectarine and apricot nut crumble with honey mascarpone

INGREDIENTS

Sweet pastry

175g plain flour

100g butter

2 egg yolks

10fl oz ice cold water

35g caster sugar

METHOD

Place all the ingredients in a mixer to form smooth dough. Rest in fridge for 30 minutes. Line in a tart case and blind bake for 20 minutes at 180ºC.

INGREDIENTS

Filling

8 nectarines

50g butter

200g apricots, dried or fresh

4 shots apricot brandy

50g sugar

METHOD

Peel and dice the nectarines, dice the apricots. Gently cook in the butter and sugar so they soften and the juice forms a light syrup, this should take approximately 5 minutes. Add the apricot brandy and cook for further 2 minutes.

INGREDIENTS

Crumble

105g plain flour

1/2 tbsp ground cinnamon

50g butter

50g demerara sugar

4 tbsps chopped roast hazelnuts

4 tbsps chopped walnuts

4 tbsps chopped blanched almonds

METHOD

Blend the flour, butter, sugar and cinnamon to form a crumble. Add the chopped nuts. Place the filling in the pastry case, cover with the crumble mix and bake for 20-25 minutes at 180ºC. Add some honey to mascarpone to taste and serve with a slice of crumble.

METRO BAR AND GRILL
73 Cornwall Street, Birmingham B3 2DF
Tel: 0121 200 1911

SHOGUN TEPPAN-YAKI

SHOGUN TEPPAN-YAKI

Whether you're a connoisseur or a beginner, Shogun Teppan-Yaki will be a delightful experience you won't forget.

Shogun Brindleyplace opened in December 1994, combining relaxing and refined traditional Japanese surroundings.

Teppan-Yaki means cooking on a hot plate and our highly trained specialist chefs cook your meal before your very eyes, using the freshest of ingredients, which you can choose from our mouth-watering menu.

If you have never eaten Japanese food before, don't worry, your host will explain everything you need to know, whether it's on choosing your meal or getting some tips on correct use of your chopsticks.

Shogun at Brindleyplace was such a success that in January 2002 we opened Shogun Sushi & Noodle Bar at the Mailbox; it has a modern interior, but has the advantage of its own Sushi conveyor, noodle menu and also teppan-yaki tables.

We pride ourselves on our fresh sushi, which has no preservatives; if you are a sushi eater you really can tell the difference!

The Mailbox has quickly established itself as a popular choice as a venue for conference visitors and the locals. Both restaurants are situated in the heart of Birmingham and very close to each other and will fully complement our offering of traditional Japanese cuisine.

Shogun is not just a gastronomic experience, it is pure theatre.

Roberto Reusello, Proprietor

Tempura

INGREDIENTS

King prawn and fillet of fish

Mixed vegetables (carrots, beans, sweet potatoes, onions)

Cooking oil

Tempura batter

200g tempura flour

1 egg yolk

150ml ice cold water

Tempura dipping sauce

5ml dashi water

1ml Kikkoman soya (available from Chinese supermarkets)

1ml mirin sauce

30g white sugar

METHOD

Make Tempura batter by mixing together ingredients.

Dip the vegetables, king prawn or fish into the tempura batter mixture then deep fry on a very hot oil (170ºC). Cook until batter is crispy and golden in colour.

To make dipping sauce combine ingredients and serve chilled.

SHOGUN TEPPAN-YAKI

Unit 15F, The Water's Edge, Brindleyplace, Birmingham B1 2HL
Tel: 0121 643 1856

SHOGUN SUSHI/NOODLE BAR

113/115 Wharfside Street, The Mailbox, Birmingham B1 1RF
Tel: 0121 632 1253

Sushi: sashami

Sushi is thin slices of fresh raw fish in vinegared rice.

Sashami is thinly sliced fresh raw fish with horseradish and soy sauce.

INGREDIENTS

Selection of fresh raw fish (tuna, sea bass, salmon, cuttlefish, salmon roe, hamachi – Japanese fish)

Avocado

Cucumber

Gari (pickled, thinly sliced ginger)

Nori seaweed sheet

Soy sauce for dipping

Wasabi (Japanese horseradish paste)

Vinegared rice

1kg cooked sushi rice

5ml vinegar

100g sugar

5g salt

METHOD

Boil sushi rice and leave to cool. Mix vinegar, sugar and salt to create vinegared rice. Rice should have a sticky, clingy consistency.

Cut a sheet of nori seaweed into halves and place a one-half sheet on a bamboo mat. With a wooden spoon, spread a thin layer (about 1/8 inch thick) of the vinegared rice on the nori sheet, leaving a little room at the ends uncovered to make a seal.
Along the wide length of the nori sheet and near one end, layer slivers of avocado, cucumber and your chosen fresh raw fish. Turn this end toward you, and then roll the nori sheet with ingredients away from you, using the mat to help keep the roll tight.
Using a sharp knife, cut the roll in half, and then cut the halves into thirds for 6 equal-sized pieces. Serve with wasabi, gari, and soy sauce for dipping.

Experiment with different fillings.

SHOGUN TEPPAN-YAKI

Unit 15F, The Water's Edge, Brindleyplace, Birmingham B1 2HL
Tel: 0121 643 1856

SHOGUN SUSHI/NOODLE BAR

113/115 Wharfside Street, The Mailbox, Birmingham B1 1RF
Tel: 0121 632 1253

Teppan-yaki

Teppan-yaki is a steel table where your food is cooked in front of you by a professional chef. You can recreate the same effect at home using a frying pan.

INGREDIENTS

Selection of fresh meat, vegetables and fish (breast of chicken, fillet of beef, lamb, duck, lobster, king prawn, monkfish, scallops)

Selection of vegetables (mushrooms, peppers, onion, garlic, aubergines – with skin on, beansprouts, carrots)

Terriyaki sauce

1ml mirin (Japanese vinegar)

5ml dashi water

25ml soy sauce

250ml sake

350g white sugar

METHOD

Make Terriyaki sauce by combining ingredients.

Cook each seafood, chicken and steak portion separately, adding oil to the frying pan as necessary. As each portion cooks use a spatula to turn and stir regularly. Allow about three minutes cooking time for each one. As the food cooks, cover with Terriyaki sauce.

Combine all vegetables in the frying pan and stir fry for about a minute, sprinkling extra soy sauce over the top just before serving. The vegetables should be tender and crisp, not soggy.

SHOGUN TEPPAN-YAKI

Unit 15F, The Water's Edge, Brindleyplace, Birmingham B1 2HL
Tel: 0121 643 1856

SHOGUN SUSHI/NOODLE BAR

113/115 Wharfside Street, The Mailbox, Birmingham B1 1RF
Tel: 0121 632 1253

THE BAY TREE

THE BAY TREE

We pride ourselves on the personal touch here at The Bay Tree; when you come your table is yours for the evening, we won't have turnovers so no-one need feel rushed but comfortable and pampered – let us wait on you hand and foot.

It's a relaxing environment, there is plenty of parking outside and our female customers know they don't have to wait out on the street for a taxi as they may do in town.

The cuisine is classical, modern English, fine dining, developed by our former head chef Andy Waters and his successor Nathan Rodgers which has really put us on the map as a landmark.

One of our most popular dishes is the rosette of beef with spinach, rosti and foie gras ravioli.

Nathan has been with us from the start three years ago, and along with second chef Sean Kyle (who has cooked for the England B football team) and pastry chef Dean Foster, we have a top team we are very proud of.

Sandra Trimbey,
Manager

Marbled fish terrine

INGREDIENTS

100g smoked salmon	8 gelatine leaves
50g salmon	50g scallops
50g monkfish	25g king prawns
50g nori seaweed	

METHOD

Line a terrine mould with cling film, leaving lots of overlap. Line this with thinly-sliced smoked salmon, again leaving enough to fold over the top and overlap. Repeat with nori seaweed lightly soaked or lots of chopped herbs (dill) or blanched spinach.

Layer inside with fingers of salmon, white fish, shellfish, king prawns or langoustine, baby leeks and herbs. As layers are built up, alternate with 1 pint clear fish stock seasoned with 8 leaves of gelatine melted in. When terrine is slightly over-full fold over seaweed then salmon and seal the cling film.

Cover with foil or lid and pierce some steam holes.

Cook in bain-marie in moderate oven for 40/50 minutes until core temperature reaches +75ºC.

Place on tray when cooked and cool press overnight.

Slice and serve with herb oil and a spoonful of crème fraiche with lemon and chive.

Trio of lamb

2 lamb cutlets

1lb mince meat

2 necks of lamb

1 onion, diced fine

1/2 aubergine, diced fine

2 tomatoes, skin off, mirapoir concasse

2 leaves basil

1/2 pint lamb glaze

Maris Piper potatoes

1 clove garlic

2 tbsps flour

Gently fry off onions and garlic then add mince. Cook until golden in colour. Sprinkle the flour over the mince to absorb the fat which comes out of the lamb and cook for a further 3 minutes. Add the tomatoes and aubergine and cook for a further minute. Finally, finish with herbs and alter seasoning.

Seal the neck of lamb and season. Place into an oven dish and place mirapoir with herbs and garlic and half the glaze with 1/2 pint of water. Cover with tin foil and cook for about 2 1/2 hours.

From the potatoes cut off four discs and blanch until tender to the touch, then fry off in oil until golden brown.

Pan fry lamb cutlet on both sides, cooking to degree of own choice. Déglace pan with red wine and reduce by half. Add a touch of flour and then 1/4 pint of water.

THE BAY TREE

27 Chad Square, Hawthorne Road, Birmingham B15 3TQ
Tel: 0121 455 6697

Tower de chocolat

INGREDIENTS

Milk chocolate mousse

3 eggs

4½ yolks

125g sugar

350g milk chocolate

700g cream

Chocolate ice cream

750g milk

250g cream

200g yolks

150g sugar

70g cocoa powder

Raspberry sauce

50g purée

25g sugar

METHOD

Milk chocolate mousse: Whisk yolks and sugar to a sabayon. Add melted chocolate, leave to cool and fold in whipped cream. Set up in moulds.

Raspberry sauce: Boil purée with sugar then cool.

Chocolate ice cream: Boil milk and cream together. Mix yolks, sugar and cocoa powder and add to boiled milk mixture. Cook to 98°C and cool.

Assemble dish as pictured opposite.

THE BAY TREE
27 Chad Square, Hawthorne Road, Birmingham B15 3TQ
Tel: 0121 455 6697

THE LIVING ROOM

THE LIVING ROOM

The Living Room features upbeat piano in cool contemporary surroundings with a colonial twist. Gorgeous chocolate brown banquettes curve round tables softened by an expanse of rippled backlit cream curtaining. A neighbourhood-based restaurant and bar pitched between the mainstream and the upper end of the market which provides quality without exclusivity, high levels of service without high prices, great food and premium drinks, with a focus on wholesome dishes. The extensive à la carte grill based menu is created by Executive Chef Director, John Branagan.

It ranges from starters such as duck spring rolls with shiitake salsa and smoked haddock and parsley fishcakes, to salads such as spinach and roquette with a soft poached egg and chicken and pancetta. With main courses, The Living Room provides a Seafood section including sea bass fillets, roast onions and peppers with Beurre Blanc, and a Mains and Grills section with a varied choice from roasted meatballs, tomato sauce and papardelle pasta to pork cutlet, grilled garlic and wild rosemary with celeriac mash.

The Living Room menus are available to view at www.thelivingroom.co.uk/menu

The Living Room not only looks and tastes good, it also sounds great with live music every day based around the white baby grand piano.

Maize-fed chicken with green vegetable salad

INGREDIENTS

1 dspn vegetable bouillon

4 maize-fed chicken supremes

100g fresh de-podded peas

80g fine green beans

4 asparagus spears

2 heads of medium size bok choi

(slice in half cm pieces)

500ml pre-made béchamel

250ml white wine

1 clove garlic

1 sprig thyme

METHOD

Pre-heat the oven to 180ºC. Prepare and cook the vegetables. Place a large saucepan onto a high heat with plenty of water approx. 3-4 litres. Add a good pinch of salt. Have a cold water bath ready to refresh the green vegetables, once blanched.

Add the peas to the boiling water first to keep the water on a rapid boil. Cook for approx. 1 minute until slightly cooked, then remove from the water and plunge into the cold water. Then remove the tops and tails from green beans and repeat the cooking process for the beans. Gently hold the asparagus spears and snap the spear to remove the woody end. Repeat the cooking process for approx 1-2 minutes, then refresh.

Drain all vegetables and place in a suitable container to be used for the sauce, later.

Place the white wine, thyme and crushed garlic in a pan and reduce by half. Add the pre-made béchamel sauce and the vegetable bouillon. Bring back to the boil – the sauce must be light, to correct the consistency of the sauce add a little hot water – the sauce needs to have the consistency of single cream. Remove from the heat and pass through a strainer. Reserve for later.

Place a frying pan on a medium to high gas ring. Add a drizzle of olive oil – place the seasoned chicken breast into a pan, skin side down first. Cook for approximately 2 minutes, then turn over and seal the flesh side.

Place into a hot oven 180ºC and cook through for approximately 10 minutes.

Bring the white wine sauce to the boil and turn down to a gentle simmer. Be careful not to reduce sauce – it has to be light. Bring a saucepan of boiling water up to temperature.

Once the chicken is cooked, remove from the oven. Keep hot. Reheat the vegetables through the hot water for approx. 1 minute. Place into a hot saucepan and pour enough of the light sauce over to coat the vegetables. Add the sliced bok choi and stir in. Check for salt and pepper and add if necessary.

Place the creamed vegetables into the centre of each dish/plate then sit the chicken breast on top. Do not overcook the vegetables.

Crisp, light, fresh, delicate flavours and textures are the key to this summer dish.

THE LIVING ROOM

Unit 4, Regency Wharf 2, Broad Street, Birmingham B1 2JZ

Tel: 0870 4422539

Salt and pepper squid

INGREDIENTS

3 medium squid tubes
(cleaned)
1 batch salt and pepper
mix
1/4 small white cabbage
1 large carrot
1/4 white onion
Large pinch chopped
coriander
250g mayonnaise

6 tsps wasabi paste
(Japanese horseradish)
2 lemons
Coriander sprigs
10 dspns cornflour

Salt & pepper mix
50ml vegetable oil
1 clove crushed garlic
Small pinch chilli flakes
8 star anise
1 pinch Szechuan
peppercorns (crushed)
1 dspn salt
1 pinch ground white
pepper

METHOD

Mix together the garlic, chilli and star anise. Heat a small pan over a moderate heat. Add the vegetable oil, then add the garlic mix. Cook for 2 minutes.
Add the salt, white pepper and Szechuan pepper and cook for a further 30 seconds.
Place into a suitable container and leave to cool.

Squid: Make sure the tubes are clean of any innards & cartilage. Slice down one side of the tube and open out flat. Scrape off any debris and rinse under a cold tap.
Once clean, score the squid on the inside about 1cm diagonals going one way and then the other. Cut the body into 3 equal lengths, then cut each length in half on a 45 degree angle. Place in a fridge until needed.

Wasabi coleslaw: Finely slice the cabbage removing all the coarse core. Repeat this process for the onion and place into a mixing bowl. Peel the carrot and top and tail. Grate the carrot on a cheese grater on the largest whole selector. Add to the onion mix.
Fold in the mayonnaise to give a creamy texture, but not too wet. Add a teaspoon of the wasabi paste and mix in – taste to see how hot. If requires more heat, add another teaspoon. Once at the right flavour add the chopped coriander – mix together and place in a fridge for later. Be sparing with the wasabi – it's powerful stuff!

Coriander sprigs: Pick large sprigs of fresh coriander to garnish the dish or alternatively you can deep fry the sprig in a hot deep fat fryer. Take care as the herb will spit quite violently for 30 seconds until lightly crisp. Place onto a draining cloth and keep until needed.

To cook & serve: Gather all the ingredients together. Place a small mound of the coleslaw mix to one side on your plate. Place half a cut lemon to one side of the coleslaw. To the other side, put a small blob of wasabi paste.
Take 4 cut pieces of squid per person and coat them in seasoned cornflour. Dust off any excess. Place into a hot fryer for 30-45 seconds until crisp. Any longer and the squid will overcook and become chewy. Shake off excess oil – dip into the salt & pepper mix, mix through thoroughly, remove and place onto a draining tray.
Place the hot squid on the opposite side of your plate to the coleslaw garnish with your coriander sprigs.

Summer pudding with thick Jersey cream

*Requires 4
individual moulds
(to set puddings in)*

INGREDIENTS

1kg x fresh mixed berries (remove all the stalks and cut to even sizes if necessary)

10 slices of thick white bread

30g caster sugar

250g pot of thick Jersey cream

Mint to garnish

100ml water

METHOD

Take half of the berries and place into a saucepan. Add the sugar and water and bring the berries to the boil. Taste the mix – this needs to be slightly sweet. Add more sugar (if necessary) or to personal taste.

Place mix into a liquidiser and blend until smooth. Check the consistency – it needs to be like pouring cream. If too thick, add a little bit of water to get the right consistency. Pass through a fine strainer.

Cut the crusts off of the bread and gently roll out to extend the size. Cut the bread into 3 or 4 strips depending on size of mould; dip the bread through the blended fruit coulis to absorb the colour. Do not leave in the mix for long, as it will break down. Place the bread into the bowl against the side and the bottom, leaving the middle free to add the rest of the berries.

Mix the berries with some of the fruit coulis (enough to coat). Add a little sugar if the berries are a bit sharp.

Place a spoonful of the berry mix into the moulds, just below the top. Place a small piece of bread to cover over and overlap the side pieces and gently push down. Place in a refrigerator for at least 12 hours to set up.

Serving: Turn the puddings out of the moulds and place onto a suitable plate. Spoon over the coulis – enough to coat the pudding. Serve with the Jersey thick cream and garnish with a mint sprig.

THE LIVING ROOM
Unit 4, Regency Wharf 2, Broad Street, Birmingham B1 2JZ
Tel: 0870 4422539

YELLOW RIVER CAFÉ

YELLOW RIVER CAFÉ

Yellow River Oriental Café-bar and Restaurant is the exquisite eating experience at the heart of the prestigious Touchwood Centre in Solihull.

The restaurant – which opened in September 2001 – quickly established itself as the Oriental food offering for the area. And the recipes are inspired by the cooking genius that is Ken Hom.

Vibrant and bold eastern colours provide the backdrop for this unique dining experience.

The innovative dishes are an exciting fusion of flavours, each individually developed by Ken to bring a unique taste of the Orient to town. As well as a taste sensation on the palate, the dishes use a varied mix of healthy ingredients. Diners look on as the pan-Asian cooking takes place in the dramatic setting of the open-view kitchens.

Whether it is a romantic meal for two, a special family occasion or a business event, Yellow River is the ideal venue. The tempting, mouth-watering menu includes dishes such as Japanese tempura prawns, Cantonese sweet and sour ribs and Shanghai-style Duck – the accent is on variety and value for money.

Offering a subtle blend of spicy combinations – many unique to Ken Hom – the restaurant encompasses all that is best from China, Malaysia, Thailand and Singapore.

The rigorous standards applied by Ken, together with the vivid reds and yellows of the décor and the attention to detail of the staff, ensure that once you have visited Yellow River you will want to return time and again.

YELLOW RIVER CAFÉ

Japanese tempura prawns

INGREDIENTS

4 king prawns

120g tempura flour

100ml water

1 egg

20g sugar

20ml vegetable oil

Red wine vinegar dip (available at all good Chinese supermarkets)

METHOD

Remove the prawn shells leaving their tails on. Slice the prawns down the back and remove the black intestinal vein. Flatten the prawns with your fingers.

Add the water, egg, sugar and flour all at once, stirring only two or three times. Dust the prawns with flour and holding them by the tail, quickly coat with batter and slowly lower into the oil. Fry the prawns until they rise to the surface of the oil and become golden brown outside. Place the tempura on a plate with a red wine vinegar dip on the side.

Garnish with julienne mooli and carrot.

Shanghai-style duck

INGREDIENTS

4 x 0.5cm thick slices of roast duck	15g onion
30g carrot slices	50ml oyster sauce
25g shiitake mushrooms	20ml sesame oil
25g mangetout	30ml Chinese wine
25g bamboo shoots	5ml vegetable oil

METHOD

Slice the shiitake mushrooms. Boil the bamboo shoots to taste.
Top and tail the mangetout.

Heat the vegetable oil in a wok and sauté the onions, carrots and shiitake mushrooms.
Add the duck, oyster sauce and bamboo shoots together with a little stock.
Simmer until the duck is heated thoroughly then add the mangetout. Flavour with the
Chinese wine and sesame oil. Thicken the sauce with a little cornflour and serve.
Ensure the duck is warmed all the way through.

YELLOW RIVER CAFÉ

42 Mill Lane Arcade (Upper), Touchwood Court, Solihull B91 3GS
Tel: 0121 711 6969

YELLOW RIVER CAFÉ

Banana fritters

100g banana	**Batter**
5ml honey	2oz self-raising flour
50ml vanilla ice cream	4fl oz water
	1 egg

Make batter by carefully mixing the ingredients (above right) together in a large bowl.

Cut the banana into 4 pieces, coat in batter and deep fry until golden brown. Put on a plate and drizzle with honey. Add a scoop of vanilla ice cream.

Serve immediately.

ZINC BAR AND GRILL

ZINC BAR AND GRILL

When ZINC opened in November 2001, it was Conran's third UK excursion outside London; with people embracing city centre living here, Birmingham was an obvious choice.

The site was chosen for its proximity to water, which features strongly in the Conran empire.

ZINC is Conran's urban neighbourhood bar and grill, vibrant and fresh offering stylish food and drink in an informal atmosphere. The food's focus is fresh, high quality raw ingredients and simple execution.

Executive Chef Nick Male joined Conran Restaurants in 2000 and was promoted following the launch of ZINC Bar & Grill Birmingham and Edinburgh. He has played an integral role in the success and development of the ZINC Bar & Grills in the North of England and Scotland. He has helped to create menus in each of the restaurants that reflect his style of cuisine, a level of individuality and the relaxed informality for which ZINC is well known.

Previously Nick has worked in Sydney and Perth Australia and as head chef of Paris Restaurant, The Leodis Brasserie and The Bingley Arms – all in Leeds – where his cooking received commendations from leading food guides and critics.

Nick's style of cooking is based on simple dishes that are well executed and allow for a touch of originality. Some of his most popular dishes include chilli squid, tempura prawns and chocolate pistachio tart.

Stewart Emery,
Manager

Chilli squid

INGREDIENTS

½ kg squid (cleaned)

4 banana leaves (optional)

1½ cucumbers

60g mooli (type of white radish available from most Asian grocers/supermarkets)

40g red chillies

60g papaya (approx ⅓ fruit)

60g glass noodles

120ml sweet chilli sauce

20g Thai basil, finely chopped

20g chives, finely chopped

20g mint, finely chopped

20g fresh coriander leaves, finely chopped (save stalks for dressing)

Salt and pepper

Flour (for deep frying squid)

800ml milk

For the dressing (Nam Jim)

Juice of 4 limes

1 stalk of lemon grass, lightly bashed

1 green and 1 red chilli, roughly chopped

1 tsp palm sugar (available in Asian supermarkets)

Coriander stalks

2cm piece of galangal or root ginger, sliced

First prepare the dressing. Place all ingredients together in a bowl and allow to infuse at room temperature for a couple of hours, then strain and discard the chillis and aromatics, keeping the liquid to dress the noodles.

Next prepare the cleaned squid. (Most good fishmongers will clean and prepare the squid for you and some good supermarket fish counters sell prepared squid tubes, saving you the messy laborious job). Slice the main body of the squid so it lies flat on the chopping board. Gently score both sides of the squid with a sharp knife. Cut into equal sized pieces (5 x 3cm) and soak in milk until required. Soak the glass noodles in boiling water – keep moving them, using tongs until cooked (couple of minutes) and refresh in cold running water in a colander. Remove seeds from the red chillies and julienne (finely slice) them. Finely slice the peeled papaya and mooli and combine with the glass noodles and finely chopped herbs in a mixing bowl. Add the Nam Jim dressing.

Remove the squid from the milk and coat in seasoned flour and deep fry immediately on the highest setting (180ºc) until golden brown for 1½ - 2 minutes.

To serve, place a banana leaf in a small bowl, add some noodle salad and top with squid and 1 tbsp of sweet chilli sauce.

ZINC BAR AND GRILL
Regency Wharf, Broad Street, Birmingham B1 2SD
Tel: 0121 200 0620

Paella aioli

INGREDIENTS

200g mussels (6-7 per person)
300g tiger prawns (2 per person)
20g crab meat
120g squid
200g chicken thigh meat
120g chorizo sausage
40g mixed peppers
20g shallots
20g red onion
200g long grain rice

Large pinch of saffron
20g garlic
Pinch of salt and pepper
200ml white wine
80ml olive oil

Aioli (garlic mayonnaise)
4 tbsps of mayonnaise
1 plump clove of garlic

METHOD

Cook the rice in boiling water with the saffron, salt and pepper for approximately 12 minutes. Pre-heat a heavy bottomed saucepan (with a lid).
Slice the chorizo and chicken into 1cm chunks and sauté in the pre-heated pan with olive oil until cooked. Add garlic, shallots, mussels, red onion and white wine to the pan. Replace the pan lid until the mussels are open, discard any that are still closed.
Add the tiger prawns, squid and mixed peppers and cook for 3 minutes.
Add the crabmeat and cooked rice and continue stirring over medium heat for 3-4 minutes.

Crush and chop garlic, add to mayonnaise.

Serve in a warmed pasta bowl. Garnish with chopped flat leaf parsley. Add aioli.

ZINC BAR AND GRILL
Regency Wharf, Broad Street, Birmingham B1 2SD
Tel: 0121 200 0620

Crème brulée

INGREDIENTS

25g demerara sugar

6 egg yolks

1 vanilla pod

100g caster sugar

300ml double cream

METHOD

In a small pan, heat the cream with the vanilla pod to boiling point, then remove immediately from the heat. In a clean mixing bowl mix the egg yolks with the caster sugar, then slowly pour in the boiling cream all the time mixing well, using a fork or whisk. When the mixture resembles a runny custard pass it through a fine sieve and pour into ramekins $\frac{1}{2}$" from the top. Fill a deep baking tray with 1" of water and place the ramekins in the tray and bake on 120ºC for 20 minutes.

Allow to cool at room temperature, then refrigerate. Sprinkle demerara sugar on top of crème brulée and blow torch until caramelised.

Serve with one scoop of raspberry sorbet.

ZINC BAR AND GRILL
Regency Wharf, Broad Street, Birmingham B1 2SD
Tel: 0121 200 0620

CONTRIBUTORS

BANK
Restaurant and Bar, Four Brindleyplace, Birmingham B1 2JB.
Tel: 0121 633 4466

BRIAN TURNER'S
Crowne Plaza Birmingham NEC, Pendigo Way, The NEC,
Birmingham B40 1PS. Tel: 0121 781 4200

CAFÉ IKON
Ikon Gallery, 1 Oozells Sq., Brindleyplace, Birmingham B1 2HS.
Tel: 0121 248 3226

CAFÉ LAZEEZ
116 Wharfside Street, The Mailbox, Birmingham B1 1RF.
Tel: 0121 643 7979

CITY CAFÉ
City Inn Birmingham, 1 Brunswick Sq., Brindleyplace,
Birmingham B1 2HW. Tel: 0121 633 6300

JYOTI
569-571 Stratford Road, Sparkhill, Birmingham B11 4LS.
Tel: 0121 766 7199

LA GALLERIA
Restaurant & Wine Bar Bistro, Paradise Place, Birmingham B3
3HJ. Tel: 0121 236 1006

LA TOQUE D'OR
27 Warstone Lane, Hockley, Birmingham B18 6JQ.
Tel: 0121 233 3655

LE PETIT BLANC
Nine Brindleyplace, Birmingham B1 2HS. Tel: 0121 633 7333

LEITH'S
Birmingham Hippodrome Theatre, Hurst Street, Birmingham B5 4TB.
Tel: 0121 689 3181

METRO BAR AND GRILL
73 Cornwall Street, Birmingham B3 2DF. Tel: 0121 200 1911

SHOGUN TEPPAN-YAKI
Unit 15F, The Water's Edge, Brindleyplace, Birmingham B1 2HL.
Tel: 0121 643 1856

SHOGUN SUSHI/NOODLE BAR
113/115 Wharfside Street, The Mailbox, Birmingham B1 1RF.
Tel: 0121 632 1253

THE BAY TREE
27 Chad Square, Hawthorne Road, Birmingham B15 3TQ.
Tel: 0121 455 6697

THE LIVING ROOM
Unit 4, Regency Wharf 2, Broad Street, Birmingham B1 2JZ.
Tel: 0870 4422539

YELLOW RIVER CAFÉ
42 Mill Lane Arcade (Upper), Touchwood Court, Solihull B91 3GS.
Tel: 0121 711 6969

ZINC BAR AND GRILL
Regency Wharf, Broad Street, Birmingham B1 2SD.
Tel: 0121 200 0620

STORE CUPBOARD

BASICS
Rice Basmati/arborio/brown
Mustard Dijon/grainy/mustard powder
Oils Olive, canola, vegetable, sesame, walnut
Vinegars Red/white wine/balsamic/Chinese rice
Flour Plain/self-raising/pasta '00'
Dried chillies
Bay leaves
Root ginger
Cous cous
Salt Sea/cooking/table
Sugar Brown/white
Tinned tomatoes
Pulses Borlotti/cannelloni/butter beans/chickpeas
Lentils Brown/red
Nuts Cashew/pistachio/walnut/almonds; blanched/whole/flaked/slivered
Coconut milk
Cooking chocolate and cocoa powder (70%)
Sauces Soya/fish/oyster
Anchovies

FRESH HERBS
Basil, coriander, rosemary, thyme, sage, bay, mint, dill

SPICES
Curry leaves, turmeric powder, cinnamon powder, clove powder, cumin seeds, nutmeg powder, chilli powder, coriander powder, coriander seeds, cardamom pods, fennel seeds, mustard seeds, caraway seeds, peppercorns, garam masala

EQUIPMENT
Recommended:
Baking parchment For non-stick effect
Cake spatula For easing out cakes from tins
Casserole Preferably cast iron, 5 pint
Colander Metal, with handles
Digital scales Widely considered to be the most accurate
Draining spoon Metal, longhandled
Food processor Good quality multi-purpose
Frying pans Eight inch and ten inch
Grater Four-sided, easy to clean
Kitchen timer With alarm mechanism
Knife set Good quality: cook's knives, serrated, bread, paring, carving, palette, cleaver
Large mixing bowl Plus smaller glass bowls
Measuring jugs Two varying sizes
Pastry brush For basting
Pastry cutters Various shapes and sizes, preferably metal
Pestle and mortar Stone, not porcelain
Rolling pin Wooden

Saucepans Aluminium, stainless steel, copper-based, non-stick
Sieves Rounded/conical
Skewers metal, wooden, Tandoori Long iron rods used in the traditional clay Tandoori oven
Steamer Either freestanding or saucepan top
Sugar thermometer Essential in confectionery and some dessert making, but also useful for fat temperature
Tins, various Metal baking sheet, roasting tin, flan ring, mould, cake tins, patty tins, Springform tin, loaf tin
Whisk Balloon/electric
Wooden spoons Different sizes, plus wooden spatula

Glossary of equipment used:
Broiler Pan containing a slotted rack that allows juices and fats to drip away from food as it broils
Cazuela A terracotta pot traditionally placed over a fire to cook stews
Paellera A shallow pan in which paella is cooked
Raciones Dishes for presenting tapas
Robot chef A type of blender
Rosti pan Roasting dish
Skillet Shallow pan with sloping sides

COOKING TERMS

Bain-marie A water bath half-filled to protect a dish requiring gentle heat or to melt ingredients without burning
Baste To coat during cooking
Bind Blend dry and liquid ingredients
Blanch To briefly cook in boiling water
Blister Heat until the skin blisters
Blitz To rapidly blend or heat ingredients
Brown Cook until surface starts to brown
Caramelise To heat sugar or sugar syrup until it browns to a caramel colour
Chinois A conical strainer
Cold water bath A bowl to plunge vegetables into straight after blanching
Compote A thick purée of fruit
Concasse Coarsely chop
Confit A sweet pickle to serve with dessert
Consommé A light clear soup/sauce
Coulis A light fruit sauce

Dice Finely chop
Flambé To flame a mixture containing alcohol
Fold To gently combine ingredients with a metal spoon or knife
Glaze To coat food with egg, milk or syrup before or after cooking
Infuse To immerse strong flavoured ingredients in hot liquid, which is then left to stand for a while eg vanilla pods in milk
Julienne Very thin slices
Jus Clear stock or pure fruit juice
Knead A technique applied in perfecting dough, done by hand on a floured board
Macerate To steep in alcohol or syrup, in order to flavour or soften
Marinade A mixture in which meat, fish or other ingredients are soaked before cooking
Napping To coat an item with sauce

Poach Cook food at just below boiling point for a protracted time
Prove Second stage in breadmaking, where dough is allowed to rise after shaping
Quenelle Spoonful
Reduce Boil rapidly to reduce liquid content
Refresh To plunge vegetables into cold water after blanching
Sabayon Italian custard, egg yolks and wine or juices beaten vigorously over hot water to form a rich, creamy dessert
Sauté Lightly fry
Sear Rapidly pan-cook meat at high temperature
Soft ball When boiling sugar mixture, this is the stage where a soft ball can be formed and squashed flat
Strain To pass liquid through a sieve
Sweat To seal in a covered pan

GLOSSARY

Aioli Garlic mayonnaise

Almonds Blanched – skins removed
Flaked – skins removed, flaked
Marcona – Spanish flat almonds
Garrapinades – sugared almonds

Bamboo shoots The shoots of bamboo plants, available in tins

Banana leaves Available from specialist Caribbean stores and good supermarkets

Banana shallot From Bretagne, where onions were crossed with a normal round shallot. Popular due to oblong form – easy to peel and nice rings

Bechamel sauce White sauce

Black bream A dark grey sea fish with tough scales, remove before cooking

Blinis Russian pancake, traditionally eaten with caviar

Bok Choi Chinese cabbage, sometimes called Pak Choi, mild mustard taste

Boudoir biscuits Trifle sponge fingers

Bouillabaisse sauce A version of a traditional Provençal stew

Bouillon Stock or broth

Canola oil Comes from the rape seed, which is part of the mustard family of plants

Calasparra rice Superior paella rice, absorbs three times its volume

Caper The pickled flower buds of a shrub native to the Mediterranean and parts of Asia

Chantilly Sweetened vanilla-flavoured, whipped cream used for desserts and puddings

Chinese wine Available from Chinese supermarkets. Use dry sherry as substitute where not available

Chorizo A Spanish sausage, spicy in flavour, made from ground pork

Cous cous A fine cereal made from semolina

Dahi vada Dumplings in yoghurt sauce

Dashi Basic soup or stock in Japanese cooking made from kelp and dried bonito flakes

Eggplant Aubergine

Elaichi cardamom Aromatic seed pods used in Asian cooking, which can be used whole or split and crushed

Five spice powder Chinese spice containing cinnamon, cloves, fennel, star anise and Szechuan peppers

Frisé(e) Curly endive, the bitter salad green of the chicory family sold in round heads

Garam masala A blend of spices used in Asian cooking

Ghee Pure butter fat used in Asian cooking

Girolle mushrooms Firm-fleshed, shaped like a trumpet

Gram flour Flour made from ground chickpeas – black gram may be hard to come by

Ham hock The narrow ankle section cut from a ham

Hamachi Young yellowtail tuna or amberjack

Jeera Cumin

Julienne Finely sliced

Khoa Unsweetened Indian condensed milk, made by cooking milk until water content is almost evaporated

Langoustine Dublin Bay Prawn, shellfish cooked by baking or grilling

Lovage Sea parsley, leaves and stems have strong celery flavour

Mangetout Whole pea pods, eaten young and blanched

Mangoes If out of season, use ones canned in syrup

Mascarpone Thick, creamy soft Italian cheese

Mirin Sweetened sake used in Japanese cooking

Miropois A mixture of diced vegetables sauted in butter and used as a base for sauces and stews

Mooli Long white Japanese radish

Morcilla Spanish blood sausage

Nam Jim Sweet Thai dipping sauce, can be used as dressing

Nora dried peppers Dried small red peppers

Nori seaweed Edible seaweed, dark green, used for wrapping sushi and as a general Japanese ingredient

Oyster sauce Rich brown sauce made from oysters, brine, soy sauce and starches

Pak Choi See Bok Choi

Paneer Indian curd cheese, available in Asian supermarkets

Parfait A custard made with egg yolks, sugar, whipped cream and flavourings

Passata Smooth tomato sauce sold in bottles or cartons

Patatas Potatoes

Peppers Pimentos – sweet, red, large
Nora – small, dried, hot
Wood roasted – traditional Piquillo peppers, triangular

Root ginger Thick root of a tropical plant, can be frozen

Rose water Water flavoured with roses

Rouille sauce Pungent Provençal sauce made from chillies, garlic and oil

Roulade Meat or fish roll, or rolled-up vegetable soufflé – often stuffed

Saffron Vibrant natural colorant, extracted from crocuses

Sake Rice wine

Sansa oil Made from the press residues of the olives by chemical extraction. Can be used for frying

Sauce vierge A sauce of best quality olive oil, lemon juice, garlic, tomatoes, and fresh herbs

Skate Flat white-fleshed fish

Shiitake mushroom Comes dried or fresh; very versatile Chinese mushroom

Soy sauce Made from fermented soy beans. Use dark for extra colour, light for flavour and salty taste

Spring roll pastry Very thin pastry used for spring rolls available in Oriental supermarkets

Star anise Chinese spice, aniseed flavour

Supremes Chicken breasts with no skin or bone

Sweetbreads Thymus gland or pancreas of lamb. Use fresh

Sweet potato Root vegetable, pink in colour

Szechuan pepper Hot peppercorns from the Szechaun region of China

Tamarind A dried brown seed pod that produces a sweet-sour paste when cooked. Can be bought as paste or syrup

Tapenade A paste made of black olives, capers, anchovies, mustard, basil and parsley

Tempura flour Light rice flour good for batters, available from Chinese supermarkets

Thai basil Purple, slightly aniseed-flavoured version of the common herb

Truffle oil Earthy oil made from truffles and olive oil

Vanilla pod Sweet fragrant dried pods of vanilla orchid

Wasabi paste Japanese horseradish paste